SURVIVING
TSUNAMIS

Marne Ventura and Heather Kissock

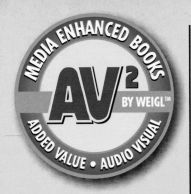

AV² provides enriched content that supplements and complements this book. Weigl's AV² books strive to create inspired learning and engage young minds in a total learning experience.

Your AV² Media Enhanced books come alive with...

Audio
Listen to sections of the book read aloud.

Key Words
Study vocabulary, and complete a matching word activity.

Video
Watch informative video clips.

Quizzes
Test your knowledge.

Go to **www.av2books.com**, and enter this book's unique code.

Embedded Weblinks
Gain additional information for research.

Slide Show
View images and captions, and prepare a presentation.

BOOK CODE

AVF74564

AV² by Weigl brings you media enhanced books that support active learning.

Try This!
Complete activities and hands-on experiments.

... and much, much more!

Published by AV² by Weigl
350 5th Avenue, 59th Floor
New York, NY 10118
Website: www.av2books.com

Library of Congress Cataloging-in-Publication Data
Names: Ventura, Marne, author.
Title: Tsunamis / Marne Ventura.
Description: New York : AV2 by Weigl, [2018] | Series: Surviving | Audience: Grades 4 to 6. | Includes index.
Identifiers: LCCN 2018053505 (print) | LCCN 2018054316 (ebook) | ISBN 9781489697950 (Multi User ebook) | ISBN 9781489697967 (Single User ebook) | ISBN 9781489697936 (Hardcover : alk. paper) | ISBN 9781489697943 (Softcover : alk. paper)
Subjects: LCSH: Tsunamis--Juvenile literature. | Survival skills--Juvenile literature.
Classification: LCC GC221.5 (ebook) | LCC GC221.5 .V455 2018 (print) | DDC 363.34/94--dc23
LC record available at https://lccn.loc.gov/2018053505

Printed in the United States of America in Brainerd, Minnesota
1 2 3 4 5 6 7 8 9 0 22 21 20 19 18

122018
120118

Project Coordinator: Heather Kissock   Designer: Ana María Vidal

Every reasonable effort has been made to trace ownership and to obtain permission to reprint copyright material. The publishers would be pleased to have any errors or omissions brought to their attention so that they may be corrected in subsequent printings.

Weigl acknowledges Getty Images, Alamy, Newscom, and iStock as its primary image suppliers for this title.

First published by The Child's World in 2016.

Contents

CHAPTER ONE
Tsunami!............................ 4

CHAPTER TWO
Learning the Risks............ 8

CHAPTER THREE
Surviving the Waves....... 12

Timeline 17

CHAPTER FOUR
After a Tsunami 18

Tsunami Tracking 21

Quiz 22

Key Words/Index 23

Log on to
www.av2books.com........24

When water recedes quickly, it may leave behind lots of foam.

Tsunami!

Tilly Smith walked down the beach with her family. The ten-year-old was on winter break from her school in England. Her family was spending the holiday in Thailand.

Suddenly, Tilly noticed something strange about the ocean. There was a lot of foam on the surface. It looked like the water was bubbling. Tilly had learned about tsunamis at school just two weeks earlier. Her teacher had shown a video about a tsunami in Hawaii. Tilly had learned the warning signs. One was receding water. Another was bubbling and foamy water. She knew everyone on the beach was in danger.

Tilly told her parents a big wave was coming. They did not take her seriously. She became upset. She screamed for everyone to get off the beach. This scared Tilly's younger sister. She went with her father back to the hotel. But Tilly's mother wanted to stay on the beach. Tilly did not want to leave her mother. She knew they needed to get away from the water. Finally, she convinced her mother to leave the beach.

Tilly's father warned the hotel security guards. They got everyone off the beach and into the hotel. People watched from above as a huge wall of water rushed over the beach. It slammed against the building. Tilly helped save more than 100 people because she knew the warning signs of a tsunami.

A 9.0 **magnitude** earthquake in the ocean caused the tsunami in Thailand. Huge walls of water rose up from the **epicenter**. They rolled over the coasts of 11 countries along the Indian Ocean. There was no warning system in place. Most people were surprised by the disaster. Almost 230,000 people died.

Plate Tectonics

Earth's surface is made up of huge pieces called tectonic plates. The plates float on hot rock called the mantle. Heat energy from the mantle makes the plates move. Sometimes, two plates bump into each other and stick. As they push harder, energy builds. The edges of the plates finally slip apart. This sends **seismic** waves to Earth's surface that shake the ground. Earthquakes happen near the **faults** between tectonic plates.

The 2004 Indian Ocean tsunami was a rare disaster. Most tsunamis are not so destructive. But they can occur in any ocean. They happen quickly. It makes sense to learn about the dangers tsunamis cause. Disaster might never strike. But having a survival plan could be a lifesaver.

THE MARINE SOCIETY AND SEA CADETS
THOMAS GRAY MEMORIAL TRUST

AWARD OF MERIT

Tilly Smith

Tilly received an award for her efforts to save people from the tsunami.

The **earthquake** that caused the 2004 tsunami had the same energy level as **23,000** atomic bombs.

In the **open ocean**, tsunamis start out as waves only about **3 feet** (1 meter) high.

Tsunami waves can be up to **1 hour** apart and more than **60 miles** (100 kilometers) long.

Chapter 2

The waves from the March 2011 tsunami crashed into houses along the coast before making their way inland.

Learning the Risks

A big tsunami hit Japan's coast in March 2011. It killed more than 18,000 people. The tallest wave was as high as a 12-story building. The water moved toward shore at almost 500 miles per hour (805 km/h). The tsunami destroyed the homes of 452,000 people. It caused a **nuclear** power plant to leak harmful steam. The cost of the damage was $235 billion.

Drowning is the most serious risk in tsunamis. But objects in the moving water can also be dangerous. When a wall of water moves as fast as a jet plane, it can knock over buildings and carry them away. A big tsunami struck Chile in 1960. One survivor remembers seeing houses float away with stoves inside still smoking. This made them look like ships on the water. Big waves can also uproot trees. **Debris** can hit people who are not able to get to high ground.

Tsunami waves can wash away or weaken concrete **foundations**. This can make houses fall down. Standing water can ruin buildings left upright. The moisture can rot wood. Gas and electrical appliances may no longer work. Pipes and sewage systems might break and leak.

The force of the 2004 tsunami in Thailand was strong enough to tip a bus on its side.

Erosion becomes a problem after houses, trees, and roads are carried away. These things help hold the ground in place. Mud and landslides may occur without them. Bridges and highways can break or fall down if the ground under them erodes.

Big waves may disable services and utilities that people count on. There may be no clean water for drinking, cooking, or washing if water pipes break. Broken gas and electric lines mean no power for lights, heat, and appliances. Police stations, fire stations, and hospitals can be damaged. This makes it hard for people to get the help they need.

What Happens During a Tsunami?

Earthquakes on the ocean floor **displace** the water above. This causes waves to rush away from the quake with tremendous power. The waves slow down and get taller as they get closer to shore. The top of the wave is called the crest. The bottom of the wave is called the trough. The trough acts like a vacuum. It sucks water into the wave, making it bigger. One sign a big wave is coming is when the water by shore gets sucked out.

Chapter 3

Tsunamis are sometimes called tidal waves. But tsunamis are not related to ocean tides.

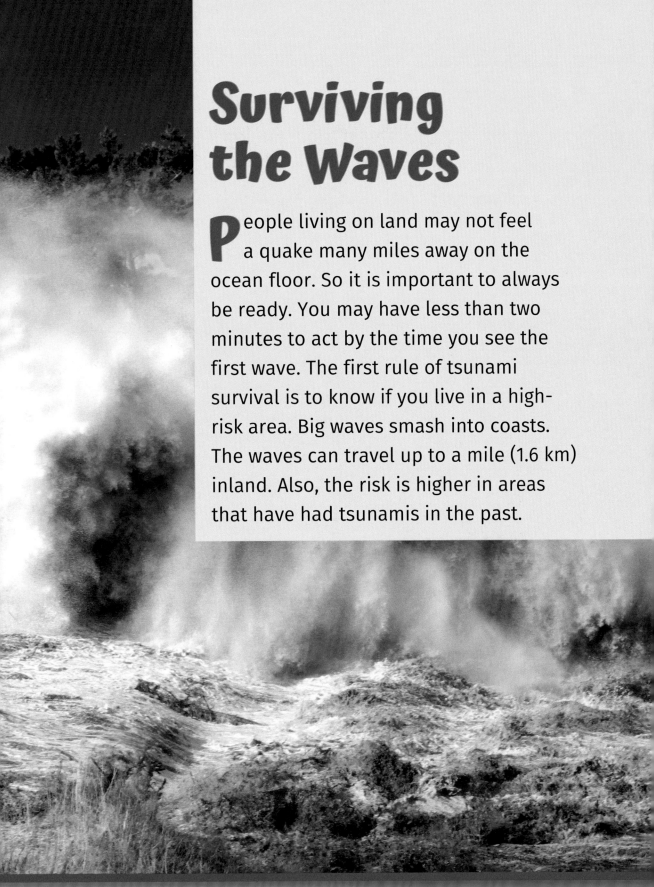

Surviving the Waves

People living on land may not feel a quake many miles away on the ocean floor. So it is important to always be ready. You may have less than two minutes to act by the time you see the first wave. The first rule of tsunami survival is to know if you live in a high-risk area. Big waves smash into coasts. The waves can travel up to a mile (1.6 km) inland. Also, the risk is higher in areas that have had tsunamis in the past.

People in a high-risk area need to know a tsunami's warning signs. This allows them to act quickly. A tsunami may occur if an earthquake near the coast lasts 20 seconds or longer. The water in the sea will go far out. You may even hear a loud noise coming from the ocean. Do not wait to act if you suspect a big wave is coming. Do not take the time to pack up your things. Get away from the ocean right away.

Where should you go during a tsunami? Try to get as far from the ocean as fast as you can. It is a good idea to make a plan for where you will go. That way, you will be able to act quickly if you need to.

Coastal areas with a history of earthquakes tend to be at greater risk for tsunamis.

If roads are busy, you should walk, run, or bike. Move quickly and get as high as you can. The top floor of a tall building is a good choice. Or go to the top of the highest hill in the area. Otherwise, climb a tree and hold on. If you are caught by a wave, search for something like a piece of wood to help you float.

People who survive the waves of a tsunami still need to be careful. Just inches of moving water can sweep people off their feet. Electrical power lines may be on or near the ground. These can cause electrical shocks or burns. Even something that is touching a downed power line can hurt you. Stay away from broken gas lines, too.

Warning Systems

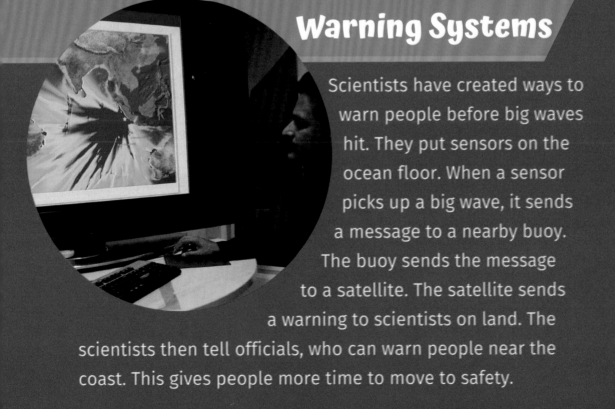

Scientists have created ways to warn people before big waves hit. They put sensors on the ocean floor. When a sensor picks up a big wave, it sends a message to a nearby buoy. The buoy sends the message to a satellite. The satellite sends a warning to scientists on land. The scientists then tell officials, who can warn people near the coast. This gives people more time to move to safety.

Leaking gas can explode. Do not go into buildings that have been damaged. Exposed nails, broken glass, and falling objects are dangerous. Stay off bridges that have been hit. Officials will let you know when it is safe to move around.

People should have an emergency kit. Pack bottled water, canned and dried food, a manual can opener, a battery-operated radio, and a first-aid kit in a waterproof bag with a handle. Keep the kit in the family car or in a closet near an exit. Everyone in the family should know where the kit is. That way, if you need to leave in a hurry, you can grab the kit and go.

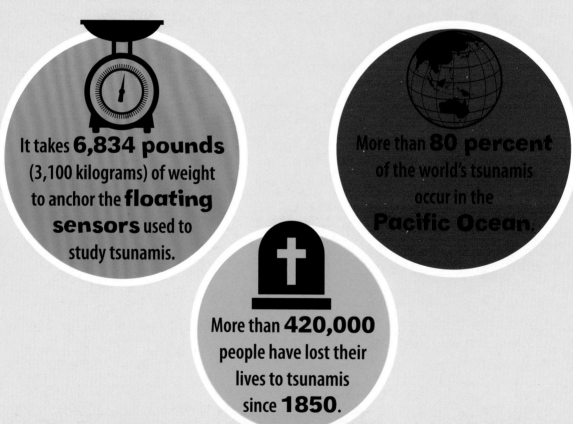

It takes **6,834 pounds** (3,100 kilograms) of weight to anchor the **floating sensors** used to study tsunamis.

More than **80 percent** of the world's tsunamis occur in the **Pacific Ocean**.

More than **420,000** people have lost their lives to tsunamis since **1850**.

Timeline

People have recorded tsunamis for hundreds of years. Many of these tsunamis have caused serious damage to the surrounding land. In some cases, the force of the tsunamis has caused death.

1650 A volcano erupts on the Greek island of Santorini, setting off a mega-tsunami. Waves are estimated to be more than 300 feet (100 m) high.

1883 Tsunamis more than 100 feet (33 m) high form when Indonesia's Krakatoa volcano erupts, collapsing much of the surrounding ocean floor.

1929 A magnitude 7.2 earthquake on the ocean floor off the Grand Banks creates a tsunami that hits Newfoundland, Canada. Waves more than 23 feet (7 m) high result in 28 deaths.

1960 The largest earthquake ever recorded, a magnitude 9.5, hits Chile. It causes tsunami waves that affect Chile, Peru, Hawaii, and Japan.

2014 A magnitude 8.2 earthquake off the coast of Chile results in a Pacific region tsunami. With seven deaths and more than 200 injuries, Chile reports the only significant damage.

2016 Photographs and thermal images of the surface of Mars show evidence of two tsunami events. These events were likely caused by meteors or asteroids hitting Mars' surface.

Chapter 4

Fire trucks lined up to help those in need following the 2011 tsunami in Japan.

After a Tsunami

A tsunami is not just one wave. It includes many waves and can last for hours. The first wave is not always the biggest. The quake's aftershocks may continue to make big waves. People should stay where they are until they hear it is safe. Officials will send information on the radio. They will let people know when the event is over. It is dangerous to return to the beach to watch the ocean. Be patient. Stay away until local officials give word.

Some survivors may not have a place to go. Waves can destroy homes. These people should listen to the local radio station for direction. Organizations that help people after a disaster often set up shelters. Shelters give people food, clean water, and a place to sleep.

Dangerous Bacteria

Bacteria are small organisms. You cannot see them. But they are in soil, water, air, and on plants and animals. About a billion bacteria live in a teaspoon of soil. Some are helpful. Others cause diseases. Bacteria need water to grow. Large waves soak areas with water. This increases the number of bacteria, which can make people sick.

People with major injuries may go into shock. It is important to keep them calm and warm.

Getting clean water can be difficult after a tsunami. Floodwater is usually full of dirt and debris. Insects that carry disease are drawn to standing water. People who drink or touch polluted water can become sick. Dead animals may also be in the water. Snakes may be swimming around. It is important to stay away.

It may take workers a while to bring fresh food and clean drinking water to affected areas. Some foods need to be refrigerated. Do not eat these foods if they have not been kept cold for more than a few hours. Instead, eat canned or dry food from sealed containers. Drink bottled water.

People who are injured during a tsunami may need medical help. Minor cuts and bruises can be treated with a first-aid kit. Do not try to move a person who is hurt badly. If phone lines are working, call 911. Keep the hurt person warm and clean. Listen to the radio for information on how to get medical help.

Tsunamis can be scary. But big tsunamis are rare. Many people live with the possibility of a tsunami every day. But they do not worry. They know they will be prepared if big waves hit.

Tsunami Tracking

Tsunamis cannot be predicted or prevented. It is important that warning systems be in place. Tsunami warning centers have been set up around the world, in areas considered to be high risk.

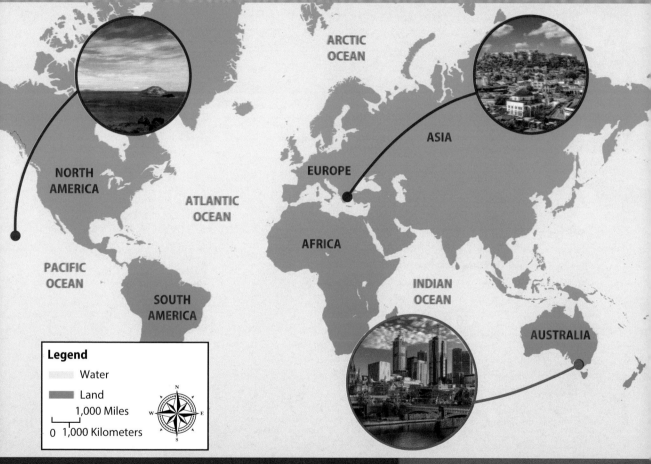

ARCTIC
OCEAN

ASIA

NORTH
AMERICA

EUROPE

ATLANTIC
OCEAN

AFRICA

PACIFIC
OCEAN

INDIAN
OCEAN

SOUTH
AMERICA

AUSTRALIA

Legend
- Water
- Land
- 1,000 Miles
- 0 1,000 Kilometers

N W E S

United States The Pacific Tsunami Warning Center, located on the island of Oahu, in Hawaii, issues warnings for the Pacific Ocean and Caribbean regions, as well as the South China Sea.

Greece As part of the Institute of Geodynamics in Athens, the Hellenic National Tsunami Warning Center provides warning services for Greece and the eastern Mediterranean Sea.

Australia Based in Melbourne and Canberra, the Joint Australian Tsunami Warning Centre works to detect tsunami activity in the Indian Ocean, Pacific Ocean, and Southern Ocean.

Quiz

1 What are two key warning signs for a tsunami?

2 What is Earth's surface made up of?

3 What is the most serious risk people face during a tsunami?

4 How far inland can a tsunami wave go?

5 What is another name for a tsunami?

6 Where should a family's tsunami emergency kit be kept?

7 How many people have lost their lives to tsunamis since 1850?

8 Where is the Pacific Tsunami Warning Center located?

Key Words

debris: the remains of destroyed objects. Water after a tsunami is often filled with debris.

displace: to move something from its usual location. Earthquakes on the ocean floor displace the water above.

epicenter: the place on Earth's surface above an earthquake. Tsunamis begin in the ocean near the epicenter of an earthquake.

erosion: the process by which something slowly wears away. After a tsunami, erosion causes soil to wash away.

faults: cracks between plates of Earth's crust. Earthquakes occur along faults.

foundations: the support structures underneath buildings. Tsunamis can weaken foundations so that buildings fall down.

magnitude: a number that measures an earthquake. A 7.0 magnitude earthquake can cause serious damage.

nuclear: related to the use of atomic energy. The tsunami in Japan caused a leak in a nuclear power plant.

seismic: caused by an earthquake. Quakes send seismic waves to Earth's surface.

Index

aftershock 19

bacteria 19
bottled water 16, 20

canned food 16, 20
Chile 10, 17
crest 11

debris 10, 20

earthquake 6, 7, 11, 13, 14, 17, 19
emergency kit 16, 22
emergency plan 7, 14
epicenter 6
erosion 11

fault 6
first-aid kit 16, 20

gas line 11, 15, 16

high ground 10
high-risk area 13, 14, 21

Japan 9, 17, 18

magnitude 6, 17

nuclear 9

power line 15

radio 16, 19, 20

seismic wave 6
shelter 19
Smith, Tilly 5, 6, 7
standing water 10, 20

tectonic plate 6, 22
Thailand 5, 6, 10
trough 11

warning sign 5, 6, 14, 22
warning system 6, 15, 21

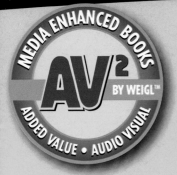

Log on to www.av2books.com

AV² by Weigl brings you media enhanced books that support active learning. Go to www.av2books.com, and enter the special code found on page 2 of this book. You will gain access to enriched and enhanced content that supplements and complements this book. Content includes video, audio, weblinks, quizzes, a slide show, and activities.

AV² Online Navigation

Audio
Listen to sections of the book read aloud.

Book Pages
AV² pages directly correspond to pages in the book.

Video
Watch informative video clips.

Embedded Weblinks
Gain additional information for research.

Key Words
Study vocabulary, and complete a matching word activity.

Try This!
Complete activities and hands-on experiments.

Quizzes
Test your knowledge.

Slide Show
View images and captions, and prepare a presentation.

AV² was built to bridge the gap between print and digital. We encourage you to tell us what you like and what you want to see in the future.

Sign up to be an AV² Ambassador at www.av2books.com/ambassador.